The Tale of Gawain

John Watson

The Tale of Gawain

The Tale of Gawain
ISBN 978 1 76109 128 5
Copyright © text John Watson 2021

First published 2012 by Picaro Press

This edition published 2021 by
GINNINDERRA PRESS
PO Box 3461 Port Adelaide 5015
www.ginninderrapress.com.au

For Alison

Part I

1

Troy, drowned in sorrows which the Past engenders,
Troy receding from communal memory,
Faint, even as suckling Romulus tastes
The salt tang of future Western Isles,

Now gives way to Arthur's reign, that arc
Brightly arrayed against that fading ground
Like a field illumined in a water bow,
A covenant of marvels, still aglow.

Arthur, himself embodiment of fable,
Calls for the singer to beguile with a tale
    For the New Year
    Their banquet table,
    A tale of marvels
    Before the feast begins;
    Yet soon will befall
    Stranger happening still.

2

Against a banner picturing boar and hound,
The festive table glows in lingering light,
Which soon will shudder at a challenger.
Arthur, himself buoyed up upon a Past

Of grandeur, gentilesse, fabled deeds,
The courteous ordering of the sunlit hours
And the bright jousting on this New Year's Day,
Delays their pleasures, waiting still some sign

Or marvel, little knowing any tale
Must be eclipsed by one who will propose
    A knot
    Drawn tight
    Which every knight
    Would lose
    Himself to unloose.

3

At that high table sat Sir Agravain,
Sir Lamorak the Brave, Sir Bedevere,
Sir Bors, Sir Galahad, Sir Kay, deceiver,
And on King Arthur's right, Sir Lancelot,

A line of blood along his severed sleeve.
And, at the King's left, Lady Guinevere,
Her eyes as grey as seas awaiting rain,
A trace of blood unnoticed on her throat.

And in their midst sat Sir Gawain, his eyes
Upon one face and form now opposite him,
    Whom
    He had not seen before,
    Bien-Aimée,
    Cousin to Guinevere
    And as fair.

4

Alone in all assembled Camelot
This Lady, darkly bright, entranced Gawain,
Who felt remote from all that company.
Fair as a summer day when saffron fields

Seem carried up with water to the clouds
Assuming there a form of fleeting fame
To gaze out from the air, she seemed to him
Like dreams he had forgotten until now,

Which wait their real occurrence in the world
Accompanying themselves. When Arthur spoke
    Gawain,
    Gazing,
    Heard nothing,
    Traversing a scene
    In a garland of green.

5

She wore a curious favour or a sash
Which fell in folds and rode upon her form
Like cormorants rising on a glistening wave.
Woven in silk the scene perplexed Gawain:

A knight, it seemed, was being stripped of arms
In a chamber by a Lady given wings.
The rest he could not see because the cloth
Was doubled at one breast. But then he guessed

This too in dreams he had already seen,
But not yet understood. The room stood still.
>   Staring at the folds
>   Gawain felt a cold
>   Presence in the hall,
>   As if all
>   This world must change.

6

A hurdy-gurdy player plied the wheel;
Its thrilling trumpet filled the banquet hall.
A singer sang of miracles, until
Into this carefree circle rode the knight.

Attentive silence, like a waterfall
Seen from a distance as the horses' hooves
Still drum on banks above the river bed,
Fell round the revellers in that vaulted room.

Then slowly from his horse that knight dismounts
And standing at the dais greets the King.
>   Spring
>   Brings no young plant
>   Nor field nor forest
>   More green.

7

He stood there in that clearing, like a tree
Arrayed in leaves; fine-tattered like a birch,
Yet richly debonair. His cloak and tunic
All were green, the green of almond fruit,

The green of limes, his mantle, too, the green
Of copper vessels buried and unearthed.
A plaited fern was twined along his arm,
A spray of lily flowers in his belt.

In one raised hand he held a holly branch
Which seemed attached and grafted to his palm;
    And in his other hand
    A mighty axe of steel,
    Quenched green from the forge,
    Flashed and dappled,
    As green as he from head to heel.

8

Lightly he leaned on that viridian axe,
While every detail spoke of a green world:
Strange entanglements, indecipherable knots
In the lacings of his garments – even these

Were touched and trailed with verdigris. Yet more –
His skin and hair alike were green as grass,
As if a laurel wreath, once gained, had grown
Through every pore, verdant like trees in shade

Whose bark puts on the colour of its leaves.
As well, his horse and all its harnesses
    Were like the rest:
    Its long mane whose tresses
    Reached to the floor,
    All were green as moss,
    As the books attest.

9

Bejewelled ribbons, braids of green with gold
Girdled that great horse. It struck the ground
With one hoof. Yet the listening silence was
The silence of the forest where one may,

By standing still, hear every growing leaf,
Each stem emerging from the forest floor,
And time seems like a branch held out of reach.
In such a silence all turned to the knight,

All, that is, except Gawain, compelled
To watch that Lady he had never seen.
>Then Arthur rose
>To greet the visitor
>With courteous ease,
>Showing no fear,
>And so he spoke.

10

Gawain broke from his reverie. He saw
A man whose height and girth were like a tree's,
A giant, lichen-green. He heard the hush.
He heard King Arthur's voice: 'Greetings, Sir Knight,

We welcome you this Christmas-tide. But mark:
I am, as you must everywhere have heard,
A modest man, but I must tell you now,
Albeit briefly, how I slew two giants,

One at Mount-Saint-Michael's where I did
That grateful high arch-angel's work and rid
    That place
    Of the giant
    Lately come from Spain,
    An evil infidel,
    A cannibal,
    And thereby
    Cleansed the Mount
    In holy Michael's name.'

11

Gawain heard Arthur still: 'I am a man
Of few words. Yet I tell you here and now
Of a second giant, he of Snowdon, slain
By me, he who would add my beard to those

That cloud-king claimed and made into a cloak.
So, verdant Sir, if here you seek a spoil,
I will serve you. Nor will my noble lords
Be lacking in the lists.' At this the Knight,

Advancing with his stallion at his side,
Laughed long and loud, and then at length replied,
    First,
    With courtesy,
    Throwing back his cowl,
    And bowing low to Guinevere
    And that Lady with the green silk shawl.

12

'I understand your fears, grave King. But see:
I wear no armour, carry neither shield
Nor halberd, bare my neck and head.
I want no conflict in your court. Indeed,

I came to you here because your courtesy
Had travelled through the land and reached at last
My leafing forest. So, this Christmas-tide
I seek a game: you have exchanged your gifts,

With kissing-games beguiled the time, but now,
Let him amongst you who might dare exchange
    A blow,
    Take stroke for stroke
    With me,
    Step down
    And without a frown
    Share this bright axe.'

13

Perhaps for fear or fearful puzzlement
The court fell into silence as before,
All eyes fixed on that glittering moss-bright axe,
And on that Knight who laughed again, and said,

'My neck will feel the first blow with this axe,
And then, one long year hence, and only then,
The blow must be returned.' Perhaps for shame
At all his brave knights' reticence, the King

Stepped from the dais to the floor and took
The axe, and lightly swung it through the air.
    Musing, he spoke:
    'If an exchange of blows
    Is what you seek,
    Then gladly as the rose
    In summer burgeoning,
    I'll open with you, Sir,
    And strike the first blow.'

14

While many ladies trembled at this sight
Gawain cried, 'Wait! My Lord!' and heard his voice
Still echoing in the hushed, expectant air,
As he leapt down and strode to Arthur's side,

Staying his hand. Thus poised, he turned and spoke
To Guinevere with all due deference.
'My Lady, what I do requires your favour;
Nor do I wish it to be thought that I,

Your husband's liege man, am more worthy here,
But is it not more seemly that the King
    In everything
    Should be preserved
    By loyal knights,
    And saved the slightest sting
    This game might bring?'

15

And then to Arthur: 'Sire, I beg you – grant
That in your place I undertake this blow.'
And gravely Arthur, sensing everywhere
Relieved assent, turned to him the axe

And then embraced him in the Green Knight's shadow,
Fringed like leaves and fluttering in the light.
'Gawain, I thank you for this courtesy,
So radiant, so publicly proclaimed.'

And then a second time he drew him close
So that Gawain alone might hear his voice:
    'The axe is keenly made.
    You strike first.
    Be sure the blade
    Makes that stroke his last.'

16

The King resumed his seat at Guinevere's side.
Gawain stood in the circle's guttering light
And felt the axe, its haft firm in his hand.
The Green Knight swept back locks like myrtle leaves

And bared his neck as stout as boughs of oak.
'We are agreed then, now at this festival.
We shall exchange as gifts, unfettered blows
As follows: first, you strike this proffered neck,

And swear that in one year you shall in kind
Rejoin me in the place I shall describe,
    There to receive
    A like blow,
    As richly given
    Full and free
    As is earned by your courtesy.'

17

'By Heaven's sacred wood, by Chivalry,
By Lady's gaze, as my name is Gawain,
I swear to honour all that you have said.
But you must name, of all the world, that court

Where in a year I'll meet the destiny
Which, with this axe, I'll shortly set in train.'
The other said, 'When you have dealt the blow
And only then (if still I can) I shall.

I trust the axe proves worthy of your skill.
I made the handle from a greenwood glade;
    The blade
    I polished many hours
    On a whetstone in the wood.
    But now, proceed.'

18

Gawain felt almost weary from the deed
Already, as the Green Knight moved his horse
Some way apart, returned and bared his neck.
Gawain took aim, his left foot pivoting,

The axe raised high above his head, his arms
Supple yet tense, a vine of energy
From thigh to shoulder. Yet his thought was cool,
Remembering past triumphs in the field.

And then he struck. The blood burst bright and red.
The severed head rolled with that impact past
    The dais
        In amongst the knights'
        And ladies' feet
        Still not at rest.

19

And even as that bole-hard head rolled on,
Budding with blood, across the forest floor
Of knights and ladies frozen in its path,
The knight plunged after, and reclaiming it

And holding it close cradled in his arms,
Leaped to his horse's back and spoke.
The face held in his arms expressive still,
The voice as deep addressed the trembling court:

'Now mark you, Guinevere, and stripling knights,
Be witness: Gawain to take this blow
    Must go
    In one year's turning
    To the Green Chapel
    All allegiance spurning.
    Many there know me well.
    Ask and they will show
    That pleasant path.'

20

That knight truncated like a half-felled tree
Which grows again a circlet of new leaves
And comes at last to repossess the glade,
Now urged his mount to rear up violently

Towards the dais tousled with bright blood.
Its dreadful rider, bearing in its arms
That precious parcel, sawed the chafing reins
And turned and galloped from the echoing court.

Some there were fearful, others waited yet
For Arthur to pronounce on all they'd seen.
    They knew the King,
    Eschewing fear,
    Would bring
    Reason to bear.

21

Gawain and Arthur laughed. To Guinevere
And all the court the King proclaimed, 'I swore
To stay our banqueting until I saw
Some evidence of marvels. And I think

That what we've seen is marvellous enough.
Good Lancelot, attend my Lady here.
Gawain, you stand perplexed. Put down your axe;
I doubt you'll need more exercise today.'

At Arthur's urging merriment prevailed,
And knights and ladies gave themselves to joy,
>   Except Gawain,
>   Who all the while
>   Thought of the Green Chapel
>   And the short year that soon
>   Would pass.

Part II

22

Gawain at last began to know Gawain
As if he had been sleeping all his life,
Or were till now another lustrous knight
At Arthur's court, whose name, Gawain, rang out

Amongst the annals of the brave. But now
The banquet board was cleared. The year began
In its own secretive, accustomed way
To pass. The first signs of spring blossomed.

The winter citrons and the pear waned.
The frozen streams were free and flowed again
    In their delight,
    Ignoring and ignored,
    Toward,
    And on past Gawain.

23

The new Gawain was like a tower wall
Pierced with slit windows opening on a Past
Which seemed to make no sense and offered strange
And intermittent views of distant fields.

One day the King announced a trifling task.
A minor dragon had enslaved a maid
In Land's End Maze. In several days the knights
Were armoured and equipped with shield and spear.

And in the midst of trumpets, banners, sails
Raised with their billowing canopies, they left,
    While bereft,
    Without reason,
    Gawain held aloft
    A heavy flag
    And followed,
    Considering the season.

24

The Maze was reached and easily traversed,
The dragon quenched and slain. Gawain hung back,
Not out of fear but thoughtfulness. And yet
The maid ran to him, not to Lancelot

Nor Bors nor Kay. Her arms were white, her eyes
Were warm and wondrous. Yet Gawain hung back.
As they returned in joy Gawain observed
The sedge along the lake in summer green,

The level of the river rushing by
Increased by melting snow lands far away;
    And nesting birds
    Darted towards him,
    Happy to be seen
    Hovering
    At his horse's mane.

25

Summer reached its high season. Warmer
Than ever knight could in these shires remember,
This weather wantonly oblivious
Coursed on as if intent to wash away

All memories. Gawain walked in the fields
Past trees of damson, heavy, dark with fruit,
And heaven-scented peaches brightly bowed,
On into lanes amongst the harvesters,

Who seemed to carry all the fields away
Just as the Green Knight harvested the days.
  Gawain could see
   While growth ring swelled the trees
   The towering year grow full,
  Soon to be felled.

26

The mirror of the woods turned lichen-green
In which Gawain gazed long, and in that glass,
As Autumn ripened, soon the brittle leaves
Were dark as dried blood, waiting for their fall.

The King and Guinevere sought out Gawain.
That Lady's grey eyes spoke of her concern.
Gawain said, 'Look! The woods speak of my fears
Echoing here. Although in autumn's calm,

Leaves whisper all the secrets of the world,
The barest branches are more eloquent,
> And they say
> That the year has turned
> To face the dark way
> To the Green Wold.'

27

Winter brought Gawain to sad farewells,
And many knights there secretly gave thanks
It was Gawain, not they, who setting out
Must find his way to the perilous green world,

A place which none had seen, none knew of, never
Found on map or scroll. A last meal,
A sombre banquet at the table where
The axe still hung as trophy on the wall,

Saw brave Gawain ready and resolved.
'Linger another day,' cried Guinevere,
    But Gawain, for fear
    That he might weaken
    And outstay the year,
    Called for his arms.

28

The grooms came early to a private room
To arm and ornament Gawain. Sir Kay
And others too inclined to give advice
King Arthur had despatched on skirmishings.

But several favoured ladies, bright and pale,
With fruits and sweetmeats visited the room,
There to beguile Gawain in these long hours
Standing encumbered as he was arrayed.

And Lancelot and Guinevere were there,
And spent some time in jesting with Gawain
>   While all the while
>   Tunics of chain mail
>   And shoes of steel
>   And cloaks and other rich apparel
>   Weighed him down.

29

In the room a fire burned all day.
The ladies handled every piece of arms,
Those layers over layers under which
Gawain was disappearing gradually –

Cuirasse and cuisses, gambeson and greaves,
Their iron finely wrought and damascened,
The cloaks all lined with fur and trimmed with gold
As if an edge of sunlight caught their clouds.

And meanwhile in the same room Gringolet,
His palfrey, dappled grey, was being dressed,
> Its crupper and shaffron
> And peitrels at all points
> Overlaid with bright cloths
> Embroidered with flowering plants,
> Doves and placid scenes
> In crimson and saffron.

30

To all these burnished and exquisite arms
Was added lovingly at last the shield
With its insignia in crimson gold:
The pentagram which Plato knew and loved,

And which Pythagoras gave his acolytes
As password to their secret meeting rooms.
The endless knot which symbolises man
After the Fall, Gawain had made his own,

His five-fold homage to the wounds of Christ,
The five pure Joys, the fingers of his hand;
>   And
>   Well might this endless knot
>   Let him wend
>   From setting out
>   A way without end.

31

One of the Queen's attendants ran with flowers
And handed them up to his height on Gringolet
Before he turned and spurred away from the court.
Soon he was travelling through the Thousand Fields,

The Field of the Lion, where Sir Lancelot
Spent dawn to dark in wrestling with the cub,
The Field of the Lock of Hair, the Bitter Tears,
The Field of Flowers, Blanchland, Hill of Springs,

And far off to the west, the Field of Grainne
And down a jagged slope, Forgetfulness.
    Soon
    All that was familiar would pass
    And by cold afternoon
    Become a strange wilderness.

32

Many adventures then beset the knight
Which he endured, his one unswerving cause
To find the Leafing Chapel. Nothing else,
No strange event along the way, no joy

Could sway his purpose or detain his flight.
A serpent at the bridge could not deter,
The hermit at the Endless Marsh, the maid
Who kissed him on the mouth and begged him stay,

Another with his likeness on a ring –
Nothing could put him from his appointed quest.
> Yet no one
> In lands east or west
> Had heard or seen any sign,
> By sun or moon,
> Of man or grotto so green.

33

Now winter was at its worst and into woods
Rode Gawain. The sky seemed filled with frozen rain.
A grove of oaks entangled in a mass
Of ice, through which shone hawthorn white as snow,

Cast complex shadows in the piercing sun.
Gold-haired Gawain saw no one. Only a hawk
Which floated overhead for company
Followed the sun. At night in bitter cold

He slept in his armour under flowering thorns,
And woke to hear wolves howling from the cliffs.
    Often when he woke
    And spoke
    To Gringolet
    His eye traced on his shield
    The endless knot.

34

Even the sky was an adversary,
And clouds in their forms withheld significance.
The map of stars which should have guided him,
The freezing dew welled up and blurred. One day

A leopard lunged at them, then keeping low,
Its head turned round towards them, led them on
Towards a rushing stream. A narrow bridge
The leopard challenged Gringolet to cross.

Gawain gave all the reins, and perilously
They passed at last into a sumptuous field.
> Beyond this field
> Lay an orchard,
> And beneath a tree
> Lay the leopard.

35

And something else was strange. At Christ's season,
When all the trees are bare, and icicles
And thousand-formed snowflakes their only fruit,
Those trees may suddenly be weighed with fruit

Down to the earth our Lord Christ came to save.
Gawain had never seen this miracle,
Yet here this frozen field was prodigal
With yellow wax-plums, shaddock, pear and quince,

And certain trees held branches on all sides
Rich burdened with the fruits of every tree.
    Surely here,
    Amongst such grace,
    He would find his way
    To that elusive place.

36

The coursing river Gringolet had crossed
Turned and returned upon itself again
To form an endless knot as turbulent
At all its interlacings as the Loire.

And yet, again, most curiously, that stream
Gawain soon found served also as a moat
About a castle on a promontory
Of which this field and orchard were a part.

The drawbridge was lodged tightly vertical,
The place impregnable, and yet Gawain
    Felt joy
    As hopes rose again
    That herein he might find
    Night shelter from the ice and rain.

37

And while he gazed towards the battlements
With loopholes high along their massive walls
Which seemed to reach into the lowest clouds,
(Although the noon sun shone now where he stood,)

He found himself from habit planning how
To rescue some fair maiden from the tower.
no one appeared. But when he called aloud,
A porter at the gate cried, 'Welcome, Knight!'

(Almost as if he were expected here)
Then vanished for a moment as the chains
> Complained
> And complied,
> Lowering the bridge
> So that Gawain
> Crossed into the yard.

38

A crowd pressed round him, curious and kind,
As if they'd seen no stranger there before.
Already servants helped him from his horse
And took his helm and halberd and the shield,

All wondering at its intertwining sign;
And in an anteroom his hauberk, vest
And cloaks were hung. Then from his hall
The lord of all that splendour came with cheer

To welcome and conduct him to his room
Set with the finest bedding, linen and sable,
> A bright fire burning,
> There to offer him
> Water to wash
> And robes worthy of him
> So to share their high table.

39

This courteous host Gawain now saw afresh,
Bright by the fire's light, brown-bearded, tall,
Almost a giant, yet most genial.
And when Gawain was robed and elegant,

Refreshed and eager, as they reached the hall
His host said, 'Sir, you are most welcome here,
And, as a traveller, you will honour us
By taking what you will of all you see.'

At this the two embraced most graciously
And lightly passed into the bright high hall.
>After all
>That travail
>In a winter wilderness,
>Gawain felt at home,
>And calm
>In this great gallery.

40

And yet some strange perplexity remained
Fringing the edge of things, as fimbriate leaves
Cast down their shadows on the forest floor.
And when he passed into the banquet hall

It seemed at first as if he had not left
Luminous Camelot. There where Guinevere,
Presiding over all the court, might sit
Informing light with beauty, enchanting all,

Another Lady was, lustrous as she.
Gawain sat, with his host, each at her side
    And she said,
     'Good Sir Knight,
     Beguile us all
     With a tale
     Of King Arthur's Court.'

41

The feast was rich, elaborate and fit
To rival in surprises Camelot.
Gawain spoke with the Lady at his side,
And waited pleasantly until the last

Fantastic castle made of marzipan,
From which a flush of birds flew suddenly,
Before he told them tales of Arthur's deeds.
He told them of the maiden in the maze

At Land's End, and the enchantment overcome.
He spoke of giants who in Albion
    Roamed freely
    Before the Trojans came,
    And of how Arthur had slain
    Some that remained
    Even to this day.

42

Gawain told further tales of shooting stars
From the blazing galaxy of Camelot.
Bathed in their glow they listened. Late that night,
When in the corridor Gawain looked back

And saw the Lady entering her room,
Attended by another he'd not seen,
Dark and hostile, spurning his long glance,
Malevolent as her mistress was superb,

Her sunless, black regard made him recall
The chapel and the axe he soon must find.
>   Yet long he lingered,
>   Sensing something more,
>   Then turning, he found his host
>   At his door.

43

'The fire in your room may need fresh life.
I'll see to it myself now, by your leave.
You must have had good reason to set out
From hearth and home at such a time, when all

Good men declare Christ's birth at Bethlehem?'
'I set out sadly leaving all I loved,
Compelled to journey for my honour's sake.
And I must ask you now before I sleep

If by some miracle you know the place
I seek, a chapel green as is its host.'
    At this the other laughed
    At his guest.
    'Why, have no fear.
    The place is at most
    A long mile from here.

44

I know it well although I visit it
Infrequently. It lies beyond our lands.
We travel rarely to the West. The way
Is subtle and deceptive. I'll provide

A guide to lead you through the plunging gorge
And past a multiplicity of paths –
So, clearly Sir, it seems you'll have the time
To stay three nights with us and rest yourself

After your long and difficult pilgrimage.
Camelot, you see, is as remote to us
>As we to you
>Must seem,
>Like two
>Travellers divided
>Across a flooded stream.

45

You must be tired. I shall let you sleep.
But first, I would exact a trivial pledge,
Not fearful like the one which brought you here
En route to your Green Chapel. It is this:

Tomorrow, rest here late while I at dawn
Go to the hunt. And let us here agree
That whatsoever each of us should win,
We'll share in equal part. There, I have done.'

Gawain is sleepy now and smiles assent:
'Good Sir, you are most kind and I agree
    Most joyfully.'
    The fire glows
    And beside
    A branch of holly in a snow-glass vase,
    The curtained bed
    Envelops him like a sea.

Part III

46

Gawain reached sleep, as if he reached an end
Of questing for that world of foliage.
He dreamt that at the chapel was a well
Covered in leafing branches, vines and boughs,

And when he drew these back and threw a stone,
The well seemed bottomless. What could this mean?
Was this place endless? Stream and sky and light
Seemed boundless too. In sleep the stone still fell.

Was this the place where earth ended in air,
Where fountains played whose plume did not return?
    Then,
    To the baying of hounds
    At dawn,
    The sun
    Spread its shadows
    Across the counterpane.

47

But then deliciously remembering
His covenant to sleep again past dawn,
He slipped back into slumbering reverie
While that fresh light, unseen, unused by him,

Deferred to him, pale at the leaded glass,
And crept away to fire the frozen grounds,
To shine through melting trees and shrubbery
Where birds were still uncertain when to wake.

Already the hounds were restive in the yards,
Chasing and turning back upon themselves,
    Eager to be gone
    When brash horns broke the air,
    Like river ice,
    Summoning horse and man.

48

As soon as dawn's dark yellow waxed to white
And they judged it safe to try the horses' hooves,
They set out to the bark of hunting-horns,
With leaping hounds like garlands round their flanks.

Deer with nostrils quivering expressed
Prescient fear, and plunged down shallow slopes,
Even as hounds swerved sharply following.
Above them ravens watched in leafless trees.

The smoke still rose in sheets from meadow ice
As riders urged their mounts exultantly,
    And into a low wood
    Followed loudly the lord
    Of that place
    Wherein Gawain kept
    And soundly slept.

49

Insofar as sleep is like a world
Between the Past, on which it floats, and some
Vague future it delightfully postpones,
Gawain slept on. The curtains round his bed

Were filled with sunlight thick as cream on milk.
And then he thought he heard a sound like silk
Drawn through a ring, or velvet gathered in,
Or as if a pail had overfilled then spilled.

Half-sleeping he looked out from that calm tent,
And half awake saw someone at his door
    Take great pains
    That she make
    No more sound
    Than light filling the curtains,
    Or leaves falling to the ground.

50

It was that radiant Lady, now alone,
Without that drear attendant who last night
Seemed like a dark cloak gathered at her back.
Gawain watched from behind the light-filled gauze

And like the sun through clouds, as radiant,
She came towards him in his tousled bed.
He puzzled at her purpose, coming here,
Who seemed more beautiful than Guinevere,

One hand outstretched to draw the curtain back.
He thought it wiser to pretend to sleep,
    As slowly she drew aside
    The muslin shade
    And sat beside him
    On his linen bed.

51

Like winter sun on water she appeared,
And leaning at his side, a dazzlement,
She smiled as he in waking slept again
In her calm gaze. And long she looked at him.

When once, by passing accident, he'd seen
The Lady Guinevere with Lancelot,
Her face unmasked and eloquent, sunlit,
As if she were advancing through a maze,

She'd looked at Lancelot as this fair face
Now looked at him who still feigned solemn sleep,
> But dreamt no longer,
> Aware only of the gauze
> Touching his face,
> And of her gaze,
> Her breath and grace.

52

Winter washes all the hills in lime
And then in water. Headlands, distant groves,
Where, hidden still, perhaps the chapel lay,
Were glittering like flint cliffs seen through a mist.

All this the windows gladly yielded up
Before she came like first light to his room
And sent him back in haste to feign this sleep,
In which he now must lie beneath her smile.

Confused, uncertain what next move to make,
Gawain lay blurred, his thought washed in that white,
    His eyes half closed,
    Their lashes trembling,
    Like a bee fumbling
    At a flower,
    And this he knew
    She saw.

53

'Wake, fair Gawain! My husband has long gone
And even now is hunting in the fens.
His hounds by now have startled on the air
The perfumed deer and he will follow hard,

While you lie here unguarded! Golden youth,
Who knows what wraith could make you captive here,
As I now press your arms against your side,
And hold you in my power while ever we

Divert the hour discoursing courteously.
We are alone. You must speak openly
    Of all you may desire
    On this great sphere
    And in our wide green shire,
    As you range
    Far from Camelot.

54

Gawain replied with every courtesy:
'I would desire, my Lady, to defend
Your honour and so doing hope that mine
Might be enhanced, to grant your every wish

And place your happiness above my own.'
'Then you have failed me here this day,' she said,
Still holding close his arms and bending low
Across him. He protested. 'Lady –.' 'No!

You have pretended not to know my mind
Which I laid bare before you. My desire
    Still you fail
    To grant me.
    I offer you that very fire
    Prometheus stole
    And still you delay.'

55

The deer raced slenderly before the hounds
At first through low brush gaining, as if they knew
Each turning in the path that soon would end.
The air congested like a lover's blood

Was thick with sounds and memories, the din
Of trumpets and the horn, the yelping cries,
As stirrups struck the horses thundering
Down shallow slopes into a dark ravine.

And there the men dismounted where the deer
Lay felled by panting dogs. Their castellan
    Stepped down,
    Bending low
    Over the struggling deer,
    Quickly to slay
    For followers to flay.

56

'Lady, you do me honour. Yet I am
Unworthy of your beauty and high state.
We should dishonour him you chose to love.'
Yet still Gawain lay prisoned in his bed

As, flowering over him, she pressed her need,
Requiring him to yield for courtesy,
All argument rejecting with her eyes
And out of hand. And still her hands held his.

'At least then let us seal our chastity
Like this,' she whispered, offering her mouth
    As soft and wide and lingering
    And perfumed as a rose
    One long evening
    In the South.

57

At noon Gawain rose, yawning, washed and dressed
In good cheer to be leisurely, alone at last,
The presence of that lady clinging still.
He walked through empty rooms and corridors

And crossed deserted battlements, the sky
A dappled and ambiguous sea of clouds.
He found refreshment, found the thoughts resumed
Of her persuasive and capricious pleas.

At length a moon rose through these drifting clouds
Above the towers where he walked alone,
> Until below, with great noise
> The triumphal return
> Of the hunt,
> The castellan
> First to dismount,
> Others bearing all he'd won.

58

When all were gathered mingling in the hall
Where fresh fires burned and tables bore the load
Of all the spoils of day, the castellan
Triumphant from the hunt signalled to speak:

'Our visitor Gawain has brought us fortune.
Winter is lean, but sometimes we may find
Propitious Nature prodigal,
As here you all may see. This venison

Should well outlast the worst of winter frosts.
Tomorrow we shall hunt the boar. But now
    To celebrate the season,
    On this day
    At our board
    With merriment
    Beware delay.'

59

Straightway that noble huntsman sought Gawain.
'You see our bounteous burden here, Sir Knight;
How well this day we prospered in the field;
And all this providence I grant in grace

Is yours in keeping with our solemn pledge.'
'Now let me,' cried Gawain with equal warmth,
'Keep my part of this bond. How well I fared,
What winnings are in full account to you

Now overdue I'll tell.' Smiling Gawain
Seized both his hands and kissed the castellan,
    And they laughed
    As they went to rejoin
    The merry throng
    With sweets and wine.

60

As minstrels played and danced, the two again
Renewed that solemn playful covenant:
Whatever Fate or Nature might bestow
On each, the other should receive in full.

Gawain then wandering through that crowded hall,
Amongst those revellers felt far from home,
And floated in these luminous sights and sounds
Like a leaf above a sunlit lake. To spend

Three days cast out of time, of which the first
Had strangely passed, and then set out to meet
    The Green Knight
    In a green place
    He had never seen
    Perplexed Gawain –
    But there, the Lady's face!

61

A hermit in the forest had described
A boar which foraged near his marsh-bound cell.
It was, he said, as huge as boulders which
Once fell from cliffs above the Thousand Springs,

And savage, a giant, ravaging alone.
The sun was struggling in those distant crags
When huntsmen, hounds and horses crossed the bridge
And rode amongst the marshes seeking the boar.

The reeds shimmered, in water shot with arrows
From the breeze. A few snowflakes fell.
    On this second day
    A deep dell
    Echoed to the sounds
    Of men and hounds,
    But none could tell
    If a boar might burst
    From the shale.

62

Higher up the hill, but still below
The cliffs and crags, startled, the boar charged
And passed them, breaking through the beaters' wall
Before they saw it fully, under trees.

It plunged strongly into the valley cleft;
Quickly the castellan, reining, wheeled and led,
With loud cries, the turning huntsmen, and urged
The hounds to follow, worry and bait the beast.

On level ground, where lay beneath the cliffs
An arc of rocks, they hoped to take the boar,
>   Which indeed was huge
>   As every man saw
>   As it stood in the clear
>   Panting, unsure.

63

Panting, unsure, it ran amongst them there,
With tusks tearing at the dogs and horses,
Swerving so that its mass felled several men.
There was water on all sides, the peninsula

Rose among reeds. Fiercely they fell upon it,
The boar, savagely valorous in legend.
Well championed by this beast proudly bristling,
They broke many arrows against its back.

At last the lord, risking the fearful tusks,
Leaped down into the stream and slit its throat;
> So that the great
> And defeated creature
> Fell at last, as sleet
> Began scattering in the water.

64

Meanwhile, Gawain in curtained half-light woke,
Expecting his enchanting visitor
Who even as he turned towards the drapes,
Was entering the room, and then his curtained bed

And gravely laughing, jested with him still:
'Sir Gawain, let us begin where we left last.
We were agreed: this kiss is courtesy.'
Her hair, as fragrant as midsummer, fell

Across his face. Through it he thought he saw
Her dark attendant passing fleetingly.
>After,
>Her soft lips
>Smiling
>Began once more
>Their beguiling.

65

'And now, fair Knight, we'll talk of chivalry:
Your prowess in the field, your face and form,
Your reputation as a rescuer
Of women at the acme of distress –

Why! Everything declares your chivalry
Except your actions here with me! And yet,
Even the symbol on your shield depicts
The entanglement of senses which we share,

Which chivalry should dedicate to love.
The very thing of which you will not speak
    Is that in which I seek instruction:
    I would offer, at your behest,
    The field and blazon
    For you to add the crest.'

66

Her face in all its lovely weathers, sun
Or shade in imploration, joy or tears,
So close Gawain felt as one feels beside
The magic presence of the standing stones,

An air of other worlds impinging here,
Her touch like that much fabled Northern cloth
That passes through a bridal ring, her voice
In laughter grave, in sadness limned with light;

All this, the luminous logic of her grace,
Still more persuasive than her argument,
> Made Gawain
> The more intent
> To resist with all his power
> Lest beauty win:
> To leave without the taint
> He desired more each hour.

67

'Lady,' he faltered, 'how could I presume
To instruct you in those arts which you, I see,
Have so refined, have so far by your beauty
Made your own that I am ignorant,

Unworthy of your bright and magic power,
You who have made desire so paramount,
So irresistible, so absolute,
So independent of my poor resolve?

How could I serve you, Lady, but from afar?'
She smiled. 'One morning more I'll lie with you.
    And time may tell,
    Or so I trust.'
    Sadly and slowly she kissed him
    As the noonday bell
    Broke off their tryst.

68

The boar's head ceremoniously brought in
Announced the entrance of the castellan.
Amidst their revelries Gawain approached
And said, 'My liege, your hospitality

Has been beyond reproach. But now it is
Imperative that I leave.' The other laughed.
'First, our exchange! For you, Gawain, this boar,
Mighty and valiant. Now, what have you for me?'

Gravely Gawain embraced and kissed him twice.
Loud laughter greeted this. 'I will not ask
    From whom you won this prize,
    But stay
    For one last day,
    Perhaps your winnings may increase.'

69

Reluctant, fearing what he did not know,
Gawain agreed and sat once more with them.
Musicians filled the hall with strange refrains;
A sinfonye so sweetly played, Gawain

Had never heard such skill, the wheel so right
In its articulation of the beat,
The sound so subtle, nasal and distinct,
As plaintive as his mood at table where

That Lady's arm entwined about his arm,
Encircling him like vines along a branch.
> They ate and drank,
> Her eyes
> Eloquent yet distant
> With many sighs.

70

'And so, we are agreed. You'll stay this night
And in the morning, as before, sleep late.
I'll hunt once more while you enjoy repose
In curtained sleep, remote from morning light.

And then we'll meet and feast and give again
Each to the other all we've gained. And still
I'll hope to find you true as you have been.'
The Lady with her Lord went to their bed.

Gawain enmeshed in doubts and fears slept too
And dreamt he struggled at the Verdant Chapel,
 Until he fell
 Under a sky of leaves,
 Where, bearing branches,
 That Lady appeared in the groves.

71

The fox was running when the castellan
Rose from his bed, as hounds and horses stood
Already restless in the frozen courts.
The sun, one might suppose, now stretched and yawned,

Well pleased to see a cloudless winter sky
From which to wait the prospect of this sport,
Where soon the fox would lead the hounds astray
Through forest, field and stream all this long day.

The sun might also look in dazzlement
At curtains drawn aside by one whose gown
    Falls bare at breast
    And back and arms,
    Who wakes Gawain,
    And smiles and seems
    More radiant than that sun.

72

The cloudless sky was like an angel's smile,
The day as if transposed from scented Spring.
High stepping Renard, red as ruby glass
Looked from his lair, a brazen thief, exposed.

He smelt the dogs before they took his scent,
Before they funnelled down the nearest track,
Howling like hurdy-gurdies out of tune.
And now the fox in earnest set about

Deceiving all his followers: through woods,
On paths below a maze of branching skies
>   He ran,
>   Criss-crossing endlessly
>   Until he threw them off
>   By mid-afternoon
>   And for a while lay safe.

73

In Aristotle's view, Geometry
And Beauty are purposive. So Gawain,
The moment she was by his side, began
His treatise, On the Roundness of the Breast

And felt that he was learning from her still
Whole libraries of subtle shimmering texts,
Illuminations rich as billowing skies.
Again she was perfumed like summer days,

Again she took his hands, and kissed his face;
Gently she said, 'My Lord, it is most meet,
    Instructive and right,
    That in this light, we
    Resume our debate
    On the subject of your courtesy.'

74

Mockingly, she said, 'My virtuous knight,
You make of virtue such a generous part
Of courtesy, your virtue brings to mind
Jerome and all those ancient gentlemen

Who slept with naked virgins, with a sword
Between them proving virtue. I propose
We play a game, and re-enact those tests,
To add flesh to the bones of our debate.'

And then she laughed. 'We will not need your sword,
I trust, Sir Virtue. I am safe with you,
    O golden-haired
    Fair knight and true
    O my paragon,
    My distant traveller.'

75

The fox still lived but ventured from its glade,
And, wandering now too far afield, by chance
Happened upon the hounds. And so the hunt
Resumed, and down the hill, across the stream

And up the rock-strewn path they passed
And often doubling back, the fox escaped,
Until retracing former tracks he met
The castellan lost in thought with sword in hand.

That courtesy, which in that house might lead
To treachery, Gawain forefended still,
    Only with the assent
    Of Mary's mercy,
    Considering the lovely argument
    Which he must hear and see.

76

Beauty assailed Gawain on every side,
As lustrous limbed as the forest round the fox
Confronted by the castellan. Gawain
Stood at the verge, the extremity of bliss.

That Lady said, 'I see you are intent
To let me languish.' This Gawain denied.
'Then have you other ladies whom you love?'
This too he courteously denied. 'At least,

Give me some token of your presence here.'
The two exchanged only last lingering looks.
    He sighed.
    'I came alone
    I brought no retinue,
    Nor even scrip to bear
    A gift worthy of you.'

77

'I beg you, Sir, then let me give at least
Some memory of myself to travel with you:
This gold ring richly wrought with hunting scenes.'
And she drew it slowly from her with a sigh.

He cried, 'I cannot take as rich a gift
With nothing I could give you in return.'
So she unwound from round her slender waist
A favour, green, a girdle of fine silk,

Depicting knights disarmed by angels. 'This,'
She said, 'will make invincible the wearer.
> Wear it for me,
> As you go
> From here in peril.
> Wear it secretly
> To the Green Chapel.'

78

So, silently he took the glowing sash.
Once more she kissed his proffered cheek.
The sun fell back behind a crimson cloud
As again she kissed him on the mouth, and left.

That was late afternoon. At night he met
The castellan who, laughing loudly, said:
'And now we'll dress the balance, Sir Gawain.
To you this single fox skin, red as a rose;

Now you must fill my coffers with your win.'
And lightly Sir Gawain said, 'All I have
   Is yours,'
   And kissed him thrice.
   'No more, no less,
   Have I won here
   In this place.'

79

He thanked the castellan for his largesse,
And laughingly declined to take his spoils.
The deer and boar and fox he'd leave behind
And go, as empty-handed as he came,

The following dawn. One lady seemed bereft,
A statue carved from ice in winter sun.
He drank to all that present company,
And tales were told of chivalry, the hunt,

Of treachery and love, until Gawain
Savouring still that sombre merriment,
> Went to his bed alone
> To sleep with fear
> And wake at dawn
> To the New Year.

80

Gawain slept while the seasons changed. False Spring
Which favoured hunting days under high cloud,
Receded like the moon within its circle,
And winter won the day and could prepare

Hoar-frost and snow for him at first light.
He knew that when he woke, no Lady would
With languishment and laughter stand arrayed
Beside his bed and, languorous, lean towards him;

Instead, a servant brought his cold armour,
Which for these three days he had cast aside.
>He slept little,
>But sighed
>At her absence
>And in the imminence
>Of his leaving.

Part IV

81

Gawain put on that armour as, outside,
The ground and trees put on their branching frost;
But none more crystalline than he, in the cold
Resolve and resignation of his dressing.

The world contracted to this icy room
Where metal breastplate, touching, chilled his skin.
Hidden from the groom, he wound the green
Mellifluous sash about his waist and loins.

A shadow crossed the window as the helm
Was fastened into place. The sun, as pale
    As Gawain's hidden face,
    Shone in the curtain,
    But no trace
    Of fire filled that lace.

82

The castellan now brought Gawain the guide
Who claimed to know the chapel like his hand.
And Gringolet stood shivering by his side,
All finely furbished in his armament.

For all of this and more beyond his powers,
Gawain then thanked them heartily. The sun
Knelt in the trees' cathedral, where the path
Led off uncertainly into the woods.

A bell tolled gloomily, as though Gawain
Already were expected in that dark
    Entanglement,
    Where no one went
    Who yet returned,
    Or so said the guide.

83

His shield held high to let the silver sun
Strike at the interlace, Gawain recalled
The Druids' Dance, where minstrels crossed their swords
And formed a star which one then raised intact.

He vowed if he lived longer than this day,
He would return. And then, his farewells made,
He cantered from the shadows, crossed the moat,
And with his guide soon vanished in the wood.

The way seemed dark and tangled. Gawain cried,
'May Christ protect us from the branching world
    And all division,
    And bring us,
    By this shield,
    A singleness,
    A peaceful end.'

84

The guide then turned abruptly and they plunged
Into a gorge. Immediately the light
Seemed half-absorbed, distracted and remote,
Unusable, so crowded overhead

Were clustered trees above those battlements.
The air was still. A stream, invisible,
Within the rock it seemed, ran strongly on.
His guide said to Gawain, 'This man you seek

Is dangerous and wilful and, men say,
Will slay whatever ventures near his lair,
    Beast or butterfly or man,
    With an axe he sharpens every day,
    And yet, men say,
    He cuts nothing green.

85

Brave Knight, take my advice. Return and say
You found the place and there was no one there,
Or say you slayed the monster with his axe.
no one would know and I would never tell.

This waterfall is where I leave you, Sir.
I won't go closer even if you will.
You'll find the place by following these falls
To others far more fierce. But Sir! Do not go!'

'I thank you for your guidance,' said Gawain,
'But at Camelot we see things differently
    And I must go on
    For honour's sake,
    As winter bends to spring,
    And take whatever blow
    Waits in green.'

86

Alone in the ravine, Gawain looked up,
Half suppliant and half amazed to see
The curious conflict of the weathers there:
While high above the trees, black snow clouds rolled

Like tumbling boulders, yet in that icy breeze
An amber sun shone calmly through the glade.
He reached the lower falls and heard their roar;
It seemed he waded through a weir of noise,

And yet he heard, as if in antiphon,
The shout of water and the chilling sound
    Of metal being ground
    On a wheel
    Which roundly drowned
    The cry of water
    In the sound of steel.

87

Gawain dismounted, tethering Gringolet
To branches leaning everywhere towards them.
The noise was palpable: the shrieking fall
Of water at the entrance to the glade,

And, spilling out, the grindwheel's resonance.
And still beneath the storm clouds' billowing,
The yellow sunlight and the shards of ice
Littered the ground. Walking beside the stream

Gawain soon reached a burial mound or barrow,
A tumulus all turfed in moss. And here
    Insistent and clear,
    Like bees in a hive,
    The swordstone rang out
    Above the torrent's roar,
    Piercing the grove.

88

Now it was time to entertain those doubts
Which on the eve of action may dissolve
The best intent. Gawain took off the glove,
And plunged his hand beneath the mail and furs

To feel the supple silk in secret there.
He did not think of leaving. Rather it seemed
A vagueness lacking focus overruled
All purpose, and he found himself dispersed

Amongst the sounds and sights of coursing water,
The overbearing grove, the grinding steel,
    Flowers growing in the spray
    Of the waterfall,
    And green moss marked
    By many paths leading away
    From the burial hill.

89

So it was with surprise and not alarm
That soon he heard his voice, echoing against
That wall of tangling sounds, cry out, 'Sir Knight,
Most humorous, vengeful creature, I assume

This hill-fort at the bottom of a gorge
Is yours, this grotto fraught with fern and vine
And leaf of every form, this flux of green
Is where we are to meet,' and later heard

A voice within the tumulus reply,
'Good Knight, you are most punctual. I give
    You warning
    With all due courtesy.
    I am almost ready
    To bring you all
    You came to receive.'

90

Then from a cleft in that fell chapel leapt
The Green Knight, glowering in a fall of snow,
Leaning as he had done a year before,
On a vast axe. His head had healed, the way

A felled tree grows again a crown of leaves.
The axe he now held was as heavy, the blade
As finely honed, as that he'd given then.
Nor did he waste words, but wielded the axe,

Demanding that Gawain prepare to take
The blow he had been nurturing for a year:
  'Come, Sir! Take your turn,
  It is the season when
  To receive
  Is better than
  To give.'

91

'Sir, keep your head,' Gawain cried with a laugh,
Despite his fears. 'I'm not about to leave,
Until, that is, you take the recompense
I promised you a year ago. Now strike!'

Gawain then bent his head and bared his neck,
So strong and tender, to the other's glare,
That knight as green as winter grass that grows
Beneath the fallen leaves on forest floors.

'Then keep a cool head, Sir,' the giant said,
'As cool as if it lay there in the snow.'
    And he raised the axe
    High in the air
    As a man attacks
    The stoutest tree.

92

He swung the axe and in an arc it shone,
Reflecting landscapes flushed with snow. Gawain
Stood grimly, staring at the distant falls.
'You flinched!' the giant shouted gleefully,

'You flinched. You put me from my aim.
I stayed the stroke because you flinched! For shame,
That Arthur's court should boast such faint resolve.'
'I shivered slightly in the shadowy breeze.

Perhaps I flinched. If so, I'll not again,
And here I swear to that,' cried out Gawain.
    'Now ply your blade.
    I'll take no blame.
    Here I stand firm
    And let us end the game.'

93

Above the Green Knight's head, the trembling axe
Against the trees appeared to put out leaves,
And disappeared into that canopy.
He leaned into the blow. He swung the axe.

Gawain stood firm and saw the blade descend,
His neck a wide white target in that glade.
But when the blade was inches from his life,
And light leapt out between the steel and flesh,

The wielding arm held back. Once more that pageant
Stopped. Snow drifted slowly through the glade.
    'Indeed, Gawain,
    You did not flinch this time.
    I'll grant
    You worthy of my arm,
    And almost
    Free of shame.'

94

Gawain rebuked the knight. 'Why do you wait?
Your blade is keen, the haft heavy enough
To sever at a blow, and yet you play
With words, and shrink back from the deed.

Courage, Sir Knight! Complete what you began.'
Once more that giant raised his axe. The air
Roared. But he brought the blade to cut the neck
So gently that a single drop of blood

Fell like a flower opening on the snow.
Gawain was startled still to live. The world's
    Great joy
    Washed over him,
    Flooding
    Like a wave,
    Grave and sweet.

95

He sprang to seize his shield, his sword and helm,
Where they lay in snow, and as he fiercely turned,
The other leaned upon his axe and laughed.
'No more, good Sir. Our game is at an end.

But listen now. We'll talk of these three blows.
The first was held back, testing your resolve,
The second feinting was for honesty,
Because you gave me every kiss you won –

For I am Bertilak de Hautdesert,
And honoured at my castle you were found
    Honourable twice
    And true
    In the matter of the kiss,
    But wanting
    In this…'

96

He drew out from Gawain's ungathered cloak,
(As conjuring jongleurs make a dove appear,
Which clattering flies to freedom in the trees),
That warm green sash of silk in secret worn.

'This sash was mine. I gave it to my wife.'
He furled it in the breeze. 'You see it shows
A knight dishonoured by voluptuous love.
For your deceit, though slight, and born of fear,

The third and cutting blow I gave. And yet
In every other instance you have been
    Faultless and true.'
    Gawain,
    Startled at blame
    And feeling, for the first time, pain,
    Blushed for shame.

97

'Morgan Le Fay, repository of power
And servant to my Lady Hautdesert
Devised our sports. At her behest I came
To test and trouble Arthur and his court.

Take this green silk and wear it without shame,
As token of the fall from innocence.
And visit us, make merry in our hall –'
Gawain declined most courteously. 'My liege,

As I have now discharged our covenant,
I doubt our paths will ever cross again.
>So I'll set out
>For Camelot,
>Better late
>For the New Year
>Than never.'

98

The sun had reappeared below the trees
Which lined the steep ravine. The green seemed pale
Beside the maze of light which crossed the snow.
Quite suddenly untroubled in this place

Gawain stood in the bliss which Adam knew
Before, alas, he saw and seized green fruit,
And brought the world the web of consequence.
He bade that Knight farewell and they embraced,

This time without a kiss brought to account.
He mounted Gringolet, then paused and gazed:
    Again the stream and falls
    Seemed to shout,
    Drowning out
    All further farewells.

99

When Gawain ascended from that steep ravine
And began his journey back to Camelot,
Spring surely had begun, despite the ice
Which hung in shards like swords in every tree.

For birds were brightly singing everywhere,
Finches invisible above the fields,
Ring-doves in hedges, or at a distance which
Lends mystery, birds impersonating birds,

Birds ringing out like bells, birds sharpening blades,
All hidden in the tender leaves of trees.
>And on that road
>Many adventures befell
>Gawain,
>Of which others tell,
>Before he heard
>Laughter at Camelot again.

100

At Camelot, the Queen was revelling still,
Although Twelfth Night had passed. And other knights
Had gathered at her side to celebrate
Before the frosts of Lent. And so Gawain

Found mirth and minstrelsy still welcoming,
Where many sought to hear of his escape
And many heard of blows exchanged, of fears,
Of triumphs, urgent beauty and great deeds.

But when Sir Kay and others were outside
He gladly told the Queen and Lancelot
    And Arthur,
    And several other knights
    Of his shame,
    And of the green flame
    Of silk he wore.

101

Then Guinevere said, 'What was that Lady like?'
To which, with courtesy, Gawain replied,
'Almost as wondrous as our present Queen,
Yet lacking certain grey lights in her eyes.'

And Lancelot and Arthur smiled. She said,
'Clearly your chivalry survives! In fact
We all should wear green silk for chivalry –
But look! How green the fields since your return.'

At Mass Gawain thought of the distant Past,
Of Troy besieged, of Rome, the rise and fall
    Of Camelot,
    Then of a vast
    And endless future, where
    All may in time meet
    Loves once lost
    And stranger happening still.

www.ingramcontent.com/pod-product-compliance
Lightning Source LLC
Chambersburg PA
CBHW070924080526
44589CB00013B/1419